# DRAGONFLY

# Dragonfly

Lara Rae

*Dragonfly*
first published 2020 by Scirocco Drama
An imprint of J. Gordon Shillingford Publishing Inc.


Scirocco Drama Editor: Glenda MacFarlane

Cover design by Doowah Design
Author photo by Teri Hofford


The author would like to acknowledge the generous support of:
Winnipeg Arts Council
Manitoba Arts Council
Manitoba Association of Playwrights

Printed and bound in Canada on 100% post-consumer recycled paper.
We acknowledge the financial support of the Manitoba Arts Council and The Canada Council for the Arts for our publishing program.



Production Inquiries, please contact:
misslararae@gmail.com

*Library and Archives Canada Cataloguing in Publication*

Title: Dragonfly / Lara Rae.
Names: Rae, Lara, author.
Description: A play.
Identifiers: Canadiana 20200199986 | ISBN 9781927922590 (softcover)
Subjects: LCSH: Rae, Lara—Drama. | LCSH: Transgender people—Drama.
Classification: LCC PS8635.A3995 D73 2020 | DDC C812/.6—dc23

J. Gordon Shillingford Publishing
P.O. Box 86, RPO Corydon Avenue, Winnipeg, MB Canada R3M 3S3

*For my parents.*

## Lara Rae

Lara is a writer and standup comedian based in Winnipeg. She is one of the co-developers of the internationally acclaimed comedy *Little Mosque on the Prairie*. Her radio plays include an episode of *Afghanada* and the series she created, *Monsoon House* starring Russell Peters. Lara was the first trans woman to host the CBC flagship news program *The Current*. Her food project PANTRY feeds people in her West Broadway neighbourhood where she lives with her dog and three rats.

# Foreword

By Brian Drader

I was first approached in the fall of 2017 with the idea of possibly coming on board to dramaturgically support the development of Lara Rae's play *Dragonfly.* If memory serves, at that time the working title was *A Life In Two Acts*. The draft I read was a fairly early incarnation in the next leg of this play's journey that started with *One Man's Show,* a piece commissioned by Theatre Projects Manitoba and presented as part of Prairie Theatre Exchange's Carol Shields Festival way back in September of 2010.

In the fall of 2017 I didn't know Lara, we'd maybe met in passing once or twice. I was fresh back from a thirteen-year stint as the Director of Playwriting at the National Theatre School of Canada in Montreal and had just taken the helm at the Manitoba Association of Playwrights as the Executive Director (and resident dramaturg), so of course I had no way of knowing how profoundly the journey of this play was entwined with Lara's personal journey. I'd been out of town for all of it up to that moment. I was eager to meet her because I was enthralled by the early material I read, and I was also sort of a secret fan of Lara's. I'm gay, and although maybe not that active in the Winnipeg LGBTQ2S* community, I'm certainly aware of who's who and who's visible and who's a force. Lara was, and still very much is, a who's who and visible and a force in that ever-growing rainbow that arcs over all of us. As a secret fan, I thought Lara was really smart and really funny and really gutsy and … well, really cool! I wanted to meet her, and I wanted to get to know her.

Say "yes" to life and it so often answers with the right opportunity, at the right time.

A step back. A not uncommon query, particularly outside of the theatre community: what is a dramaturg? Great question! In

Canada, we haven't even settled on how to pronounce or spell it yet ("dramaturg" with a hard "g," or "dramaturge" with a soft "g" … both are acceptable, and both are used, with regional preferences across the country). And our nation's version of dramaturgy is somewhat unique too, on the world stage. Our version is most commonly understood to mean someone who works directly with the playwright, helping them to develop their play through conversation and consultation and feedback and questions, while shaping and guiding the development process as a whole.

The relationship between playwright and dramaturg is very personal, and is built on deep and (hopefully) unshakeable trust. As dramaturg, I'm the playwright's best buddy, I'm the developing play's audience from draft to draft, I'm sometimes the unforgiving and relentless taskmaster (i.e., both good cop and bad cop), I'm the storyteller's confidante, I'm often one of the conduits for communication between members of the artistic team, and in Lara's case (I LOVE her for calling me this)… "the trans whisperer." She said it, I didn't! Always with a joke, our Ms. Rae.

When one is working dramaturgically with a playwright on the development of their play, particularly one that leans heavily into autobiography, there is no topic that is out of bounds. And every story, every offer of material, every draft … the dramaturg must believe in it as much as the playwright. It has to be as real for me as it is for the storyteller, if I'm to be of any service to them.

So, yeah, meetings and chats are required before agreeing to embark on that kind of journey, for the sake of both the dramaturg and the playwright. It has to be a good fit.

I've never confirmed this with Lara, but I think we were both kind of nervous at that first meeting. I certainly was. Nerves born of wanting the meeting to go well, because I really wanted to do this. And it did go well. Lara leaned into her wicked sense of humour, which I've come to learn is her icebreaker, her way of relaxing people, and (sorry, Lara, but it's true) sometimes her way of getting people onside when she needs them onside. And I took every opportunity to show off and let her know how deeply and thoroughly I'd read the early material she'd sent to me, and how excited I was by it and how onside I was with her early instincts. We buttered each other's toast at every opportunity, and it was crystal clear by the end of our first meeting that we were both all in.

And what a lovely, profound, and compelling decision that turned out to be. I just checked my *Dragonfly* folder. Over one hundred documents. Of course those aren't all drafts (although quite a few of them are!). The documents represent the journey captured on digital paper; some drafts, yes, but mostly scenes, notes, and lots of "Brian can you have a look at this" jottings and thoughts. Hours and hours of face time and phone conversations and emails distilled into digital story offers.

It was the face time that had the most impact on me. Being invited into Lara's life and mind and heart is a privilege. She's an old soul with a young spirit (my favourite combination) and is a fearless and gifted and thoroughly entertaining storyteller in person. And the breadth and depth of her remarkable career has left her well-armed and well-equipped to meet the demands of offering up incredibly vulnerable and personal material for discussion. And discuss we did; what-ifs, questions, offers, challenges, revisiting earlier material, imagining new material that hadn't been considered yet, going off on spectacular riffs that had nothing to do with the project at hand, talking about literature and art, swapping early tales of formative events in each of our lives, and … yes … gossiping a bit too.

And then Lara would go off on her own again, and write, and come back with something entirely different than what we'd talked about. And I couldn't have been more delighted. A dramaturg's dream playwright is one that listens and hears and then goes away and makes it their own.

There were lots of marked and pointed breakthroughs along the way. Realizing that it was a one-act play vs. a two-act play, a huge leg up towards understanding the structure of this piece. Realizing that the two voices weren't two separate voices defined by gender, but rather two incarnations of a single, unique, individual voice. They and Them. Realizing that yes, indeed, we needed to bow, or at least curtsy, to the chronology of time to capture this life journey (both she and I certainly fought that for many drafts before buckling). And a profound, and I would offer, difficult, choice concerning when this particular story would "end." It's still an ongoing story for Lara, but the play itself and the story it contained had to end somewhere. For me, as a dramaturg, those breakthroughs and others became the touchstones in my memory of the development process.

But beyond the marked and pointed breakthroughs, my most compelling memories are steeped in witnessing the constant ebb and flow of a storyteller wrestling their own life's experience into dramatic form. No small feat, as Aristotle first mused thousands of years ago in his *Poetics*, contemplating the life story of Heracles. Lara and I often returned to the idea that Truth is more important than Facts, that unity of story is not the same as the unity of one's life, that some of our most potent life memories and events aren't necessarily the most informative or impactful or dramatically significant from an audience point of view.

One of the most courageous theatrical choices Lara made, in my opinion, was committing her story to play form using blank verse, with nary a stage direction in sight. For those outside of the theatre community, I can assure you this is a leap of faith of the highest order in one's artistic collaborators. It is not only blank verse, it is a blank canvas, from a production point of view. What theatrical world does this live in? How to stage it? How to design it? What are we hearing outside of the actors' voices? What are the costumes? Are there props? Etc etc etc etc. Lara has provided, in the purest sense of the word, a blueprint that relies on the hearts and minds and imaginations of a visionary director, a dream team of designers (lighting, set, costume, sound), and two highly skilled and talented actors to lift her brilliant verse off the page and manifest it as a production in a theatre. This is the play's challenge, and for the right team, this is its gift. The premiere workshop production at Theatre Projects Manitoba and the team behind it certainly answered that challenge, and it was largely because they relished in the gift that Lara had given them.

I'm going to be bold and speak on Lara's behalf, and hopefully I've got this right. Trust me, a year and a half into working with Lara on this play, and there were all sort of things I was still getting wrong. I thank her for her patience in that regard. But I'm going to take a stab at this one, and hopefully I've got it right –

*Dragonfly* is not an attempt to capture the trans journey. It is an attempt to capture Lara's journey as a trans woman. From the get-go, her desire was to share her individual truth in a dramatic form, with no aspirations of speaking to the larger thematic. But the specific does release the universal, at least to a certain degree. There are aspects of the trans journey that I, as a cisgender gay man, understand more deeply for having worked with Lara, and for having experienced that particular thread of her personal story as told in this play. Our shared humanity is anchored in our common emotional terrain, not our intellectual preoccupations and proclivities. We are connected, as human beings, by our hearts, not our minds. My heart understands my trans sisters and brothers better for working on this piece, and for the play that resulted from that work, and I thank Lara for that.

Enjoy.

*Brian Drader is the Executive Director of the Manitoba Association of Playwrights.*

# Production History

*Dragonfly* had its workshop production premiere at the Rachel Browne Theatre, March 14th, 2019, produced by Theatre Projects Manitoba.

THEY ............................................ Sarah Constible
THEM ..................................................... Eric Blais
Directed by ................................... Ardith Boxall
Dramaturg ..................................... Brian Drader
Production Designer ............... Hugh Conacher
Costume Designer .................. Maureen Petkau
Sound Design & Composer .... Emma Hendrix
Production Manager ....... Steven Vande Vyvere
Stage Manager ........................ Michael Duggan

A previous, shorter, one-actor version of this work titled *One Man's Show* debuted Sept 25th, 2010, starring Sarah Constible. Both works were commissioned by Theatre Projects Manitoba.

## A Note on the Text

I have named the characters THEY and THEM to keep binary categories out of the equation. While the original production had a cis male and female actor, this is not a preference. The desire of the work is to depart from the obsession with trans bodies and to hear in conversation the inside voice of a trans person from childhood to medical transition. It is a work for two actors but beyond that, be free.

Descriptions of trans personhood are those experienced by the author and are in no way meant to be taken as universal.

While this is a biographical work it is also, as such, solely the product of the author's imagination.

SECTION 1:
**INNOCENCE**

**1.**

THEY: Tragically, surrounded by family and friends, after a courageous battle, I was born.

THEM: My mother wanted a girl. She'd have to wait two years.
Before my sister was born, she had me.

THEY: They called me Adam.

THEM: She wanted a girl. And there *I* was.
Just lying there like a lump.

THEY: *You're lazy, that's your problem.*

THEM: There I was. I've been here ever since.
I was yellow when I came out. Like a yolk, still runny.
They put me in a metal pan: under the easy bake bulb.
I turned over: from yellow to red.
A sheet of glass: a metal bed.

THEY: Alone. Surrounded by family and friends.

**2.**

THEM: Glasgow: 1963.

THEY: I was born on payday.

THEM: *The wages of sin are birth.*

THEY: Protestant or Catholic?

THEM: Atheist!

THEY: Protestant atheist or Catholic atheist?

THEM: Born with nothing but a religion.
Not that they needed to write it down.
If I'd been Catholic, I'd have been born on the other side, in *their* hospital.

THEY: Under an anorexic Jesus. Brass; cast on ruddy wood. Give him *my* milk. Dip it in a dirty sponge. Put it to *his* lips. They gave him vinegar. Stinging his cuts.

THEM: But he was a big boy, so he didn't cry.

THEY: He was a *good* boy and he didn't cry. And even though he was big, his ma could hold him in her arms like a baby. Rocking him like a wee baby.

THEM: Though he was big, she held him in her arms.

THEY: Cradled big Jesus in her arms. I love you, always.

THEM: He was a man, but she held him like her wee boy.

THEY: And it was okay. Because he was dead.

THEM: *Healing the sick with sawdust hands, dead skin cells fell, like soft pink rain.*

*Beat.*

## 3.

THEM: I shut my eyes in the boxed-in backyard of the *close* in Glasgow where we lived as a family. My mum, my dad, my sister and.

THEY: I shut them tight, my four-year-old eyes. My fat fists clench.

THEM: And I bear down: you can do it.
Push-push, Adam.
Push down.
Bear down.

THEY: With four-year-old, force and fury, I fully felt, that by some miracle, on unfolding my eyes –

THEM: – opening them for the first time, to a brighter world. That I would become –

THEY: That I would.

THEM: That I would become.

THEY: I want. I just want. I just want to be.

THEM: A girl; a girl; a girl; a girl.

**4.**

THEM: I climb into the crib. I am two. I am robust. I am not a sickly child. I am no longer an only child. I take her neck with my fat soft hands. I choke her. My father pulls me off. My sister didn't cry. I had her alone for about a minute.

THEY: It was a big family joke.

**5.**

THEM: I am four—

THEY: five, six—

THEM: Seven years old, standing in the closet.
Two rows of clothes hang on a bar.

THEY: One row is for my sister.

THEM: The other …

THEY: Standing in the walk-in wardrobe, my hand shakes. I stretch on tiptoes for the metal hanger.

THEM: My hand bunches a girl's dress.
I pull it quickly over my head and yank down.

THEY: My heart hammers. I taste metal.

THEM: I stand up straight and close my eyes.
I wish, I could just.

THEY: I wish I could just,

THEM: I wish I could just, be.

## 6.

THEM: Before bed, Mum rubs medicine on my elbows.
Psoriasis; warts.

THEY: It's the bad coming out, she says.

THEM: Every eruption, every unsettling, makes Mum scared.

THEY: And me as well.

THEM: So that often, I wet the bed.

THEY: *(Sings.)*
Jesus Loves Me
This I know. For the Bible tells me so

THEM: Circular Reasoning.

*Beat.*

THEY: Adam was so slow to walk, my mother says, we thought we would have to push him to school in a pram.

THEM: She tells everyone, so I know it must be bad.

*Beat.*

THEY: Beside the bed, Mum reads me stories.

THEM: Looking tired, she tucks me in.
When it's dark, people walk by,
Rattling our basement window.
Hard soles, echo on the pavement.

THEY: The slapping frightens me.

THEM: And the loud, drunk shouts.

THEY: I blink my eyes, on and off, on and off, on and off.

*Beat.*

THEM: On the top bunk, I hide my special hankie.
Sewn in red in the corner, the letter A.

THEY: *They called me Adam.*

THEM: Real hankies make you big, hankies are for Gentlemen:

THEY: Gents, like it says on the toilet door.

THEM: At night, I put the hankie in my bum.

THEY: The hankie, once white, is covered with brown spots. Like a cow.

THEM: I hold it to my face in the dark, and breathe in the newest smell.

THEY: And then – I am calm.

*Beat.*

THEM: On some nights, I hear the click, click of heels
And happy laughs.

THEY: The clicking echo comforts me.

THEM: Happy girls in coats walk arm in arm.

THEY: And sometimes, they smoosh together.

Sarah Constible (They), Eric Blais (Them), Theatre Projects Manitoba, March, 2019.
*Photo by Leif Norman.*

THEM: Their shoulders lean so close, they almost tumble over.

THEY: And then, they laugh some more.

THEM: When people touch me, I jump. When people clap or bang a nail, I blink my eyes.

THEY: On and off, on and off, on and off.

**7.**

THEM: Now, it's daytime, but Dad is in bed.
Cheeks caved, he opens his mouth and blood pours out –

THEY: – red wine, into a silver pan.

THEM: Mom comes to empty it.

THEY: She is twenty-four. Dad is twenty-eight.

THEM: Later, when Dad gets his new false teeth, he builds us a swing.
It hangs on ropes in the kitchen doorway.

THEY: I swing, or push my sister, while mince hisses in the pan.

*Beat.*

THEM: I am a boy on the outside, but never an outside boy.

THEY: The green grass terrifies me. The smell. And how, when the sun comes up, the whole backyard would sweat.

THEM: My mother takes me outside and puts me down.

THEY: Go play, she says, and plunks me down on the spongy wet lawn.

THEM: I sit on the too green grass watching my mother rock my sister, barred from them by a low fence of wrought-iron pikes. Envy green, I shake the bars, on fire with five-year-old fury.

THEY: Locked out, barred, panic burns me inside, burns me inside out.

## 8.

THEM: When the time comes for school, I don't need a pram. I am big and cross the Clyde River.

THEY: I am big, and Mum holds my hand.

THEM: Homelea Primary School, established 1907.

THEY: Dunce cap, belt and cane.

THEM: There's an entrance for boys.

THEY: And an entrance for girls. We march in uniform like soldiers.

THEM: It is September. 1968. Above the waist, our uniforms are the same.

THEY: Above the waist, we are the same.

THEM: Green cap, green jacket,

THEY: grey trousers.

THEM: How I want that grey skirt.

THEY: As we march in, a tiny child, at a chipped piano, bangs out Heart and Soul.

THEM: With neither heart nor soul.

*Beat.*

THEY: At recess, we march into our separate yards.
Matrons blow whistles.

THEM: I blink my eyes.

THEY: On and off. On and off. On and off.

THEM: Glasgow: City of Whistles.
Whistles: From the ceramic factory down the road.
From the workmen: whistles, as girls walk by.
And endless whistles from the football pitch.

THEY: And from a hundred thousand kettles.

THEM: For a million cups of tea.

*Beat.*

THEY: *Wheep! Wheep! Wheep!* shrieks the matron's whistle.
Boys, over there.

THEM: Girls, over there!

THEY: You, Adam! Over there!

THEM: I hold the wrought-iron bars; stare into the girls' yard.
And the matron says: Who's yer girlfriend then?

THEY: And I only want to cry.

THEM: And I only want to die.

**9.**

THEM: Stealing a ring from my sister's jewellery box. A plastic jewel set in a band of plastic gold.

THEY: It's not for me.

THEM: I drop it in the dried, black inkwell of her cracked, wooden desk.
The girl I want to be friends with.

THEY: The girl I want to be.

THEM: When I walk past her desk the next day, my pulse tickles the bottom of my feet.

THEY: The ring is gone.
I will never see it again.

THEM: Later, I lift the lid of my small wooden desk. My thumb strokes the wart on my index finger. I take the compass point and jam it into the flat, rubbery bump.

THEY: Blood sprays from the burst. Like a fountain.

*Beat.*

THEM: When the school took us to church, it was November 11. The noisy boys bother me and the old men with medals scare me. Their jackets are too big.

THEY: They look like old children.

THEM: One boy makes the poppy petals into lips like a girl's. The girls laugh. The boys laugh.

THEY: Adam laughs.

THEM: A bad boy makes a loud noise like a machine gun. The teacher hits him.

THEY: She tells us we need to be sad.

THEM: The minister has a son. But he is a man and has hooks for hands.

THEY: I want to touch them to see if they're cold.

**10.**

THEM: I stand at a corner. On a wet, grey afternoon on Sauchiehall St., Glasgow. With my mother and her friend.

THEY: Like her, no more than twenty-six.

THEM: Who asks, no more than seven-year-old me:

THEY: Who you going to marry then?

THEM: And I say to both women:

THEY: Girls really, pimpled, in too tight shoes –

THEM: Seven-year-old me says:

THEY: I will *marry* my best friend David O'Grady!

THEM: Mum stops smiling. And looks old.

THEY: Boys cannee marry boys then, Adam, she says.

THEM: I have rained on the day.

**11.**

THEM: When we meet Granny for empire biscuits and high tea at the Grand Central Station Hotel, I smell the perfume and smoke. The imperial windows are as tall as trees.

THEY: How do you make a Venetian blind?

THEM: Poke his eyes out.

THEY: I play with the long nylon string.

THEM: The nylon cord of the blind goes around and around and around my neck. And when I move my head;

BOTH: a click.

THEM: And then, like a seesaw,

THEY: or a guillotine.

THEM: The heavy blind unfurls, headlong, and accordions down the smooth, glass pane.

THEY: Rips and rattles heavily down, with a slatty, clackity, zip.

THEM: From across the dining room, you can almost *hear* the woman pointing.

THEY: I quickly rise out of my chair. Yanked up;

BOTH: hanged by the neck.

THEM: A big man with big scissors comes bounding over and cuts the cord.

THEY: A backwards lasso frees my pudgy neck.

THEM: The twirling cord describes circles over my head,

BOTH: like a halo.

THEM: The big man laughs:

THEY: The wee lad nearly went to the gallows, without a peep.

THEM: I was a quiet child.

THEY: You could take me anywhere.

## 12.

THEM: After Christmas comes Hogmanay, and my parents are going to a party.
On the BBC, they announce that an actor on my favourite TV show is dead. He was Smith from *Alias Smith and Jones.*

THEY: He played a cowboy. Shot himself in the head.

THEM: I go into their room to tell Mum and Dad. I feel big telling them.

THEY: Didn't tell them you liked him, did ya?

THEM: I thought he was handsome.

THEY: *Boys' cannee marry boys, Adam.*

## 13.

THEY: On July 14th, 1972, we move to Canada.

BOTH: I don't sleep.

THEY: I have a plastic Mountie near my bed.

THEM: But now, I will see a real Mountie and get a chopper bicycle.

THEY: Before we leave, I flush my special hankie down the toilet. The toilet clogs, and I close the door. Now, there is nothing left. Every room is empty.

THEM: There are holes in the kitchen doorway where Dad hung the swing.

THEY: Bye house, we said, and Dad locked the door.

*Beat.*

THEM: David O'Grady came to the airport with his mum, to see me off.

THEY: Isn't that a nice surprise for you? said my mum.

THEM: David wears a tie. His hair is slicked down. We have good shoes and my sister wears a dress. It spills from her tummy like an umbrella.

THEY: Shake hands, we are told.

THEM: David and I shake hands and hug.

THEY: I can smell his neck.

BOTH: Soap.

THEM: I want to kiss him. I like his face. His hand is soft, small, pink, and damp.

BOTH: *Boys cannee marry boys…*

THEY: My cheeks are Celtic and ruddy, and my legs are strong and fat.

THEM: Soon, I will narrow, stretch and brown. Like a hide.

## 14.

THEM: In Canada, the summers are long, and our building has a pool. Now that I'm eleven I can swim.

THEY: My body is brown and baked by the sun. I have a chopper bike and my very own room.

THEM: I take a rubber band I have been looping on my finger.

THEY: As eleven-year-olds do.

THEM: I pull down my swim trunks. A plastic anchor and a chain on the front.
Dad-style sailor trunks, but boy-sized. Square-legged, before Speedos were the rage.

THEY: I am skinny and brown. And below the trunk line:
I am white, so white.

THEM: The door doesn't lock. I roll the rubber band down over my thing.
And I loop it. And I roll down.

THEY: And I think, like a condom.
But I don't want to think of condoms.
This was 1974. I no longer close my eyes and bear down hard.
Or wish. Or want. Or feel.

THEM: But now I have hope. And I roll down. The elastic band is tight.

BOTH: Like a tourniquet.

THEM: And once that tight band strangles the base, like mercury rising, my thing swells full of blood.

BOTH: Like a bedbug. Or a tick.

THEM: But now it is purple. And I sense trouble.

THEY: Ow. Ow. Ow.

THEM: I sense movement in the house. I try to roll up the rubber band, but it is too tight.

THEY: Ow. Ow. Ow.

THEM: I take the house key which hangs from a ribbon round my neck. And I slide it sideways under the bundled band. And I saw.

THEY: The key's dull teeth work the band.

BOTH: Ow. Ow. Ow.

THEM: And the key's dull bottom worries the skin below.

BOTH: Ow. God. Ow.

THEM: When sawing fails, I yank the key like a chainsaw cord. Single bands snap, one by one.

THEY: Ping. Ping. Ping.

THEM: Then, with a sad flourish –

THEY: a shameful, eleven-year-old Houdini –

THEM: I escape.

THEY: Raw and sore is the gash. For a day or two, I worry about gangrene.

THEM: It throbs angrily and aches for a week.

THEY: Then,

THEM: one day,

THEY: it is like it never happened.

## 15.

THEY: At my new school, Forest Manor Public School, the bathroom game was tricky.
Picture it. My hand lurching up, the frustration on the teacher's face:
I made you all go at recess. In you went, Adam, with the rest of the boys.

THEM: How could she know?

THEY: As the other boys elbowed by to drain their whistles, that I would not stand for it. I could not stand for it.

THEM: I held everything in.

THEY: And she, with much chagrin and a dismissive wave, sent me off to try again. And I would feel a flush, as I passed the boys' room on the second floor.

THEM: And the girls' room on the second floor. And I'd push open the double doors of the stairwell.

THEY: And down to the main floor, past the office.

THEM: Don't get caught.

THEY: Now, I run fast and hard. And the floor gleams and the building turns.
And behind the wall that my fingers dance along: the quiet gym.

THEM: Inside the gym is a bathroom for the boys. And a bathroom for the girls.

THEY: But the boys' bathroom is special. It has no urinal.
Just a sink and a single stall.

THEM: It looks like a BOYS on the outside.

THEY: But like a GIRLS on the inside.

THEM: And was, where at ten years old,

THEY: and eleven too, and barely twelve,

THEM: I lock that stall door and sit to pee.

THEY: And feel, in my whole self – before the dam bursts:

THEM: Complete, overwhelming serenity.

**16.**

THEY: At night, Mum works at Simpsons. She works in the china department. She brings us to work and buys us comics. I want Supergirl but choose Batman. My sister and I sit on stepladders in the stockroom. Don't touch anything, Mum says.

THEM: On TV, Batman is handsome, but Robin is annoying. The show is on channel 29 from Buffalo. It is the best channel. *Little House on the Prairie, Superman,* and *Leave it to Beaver.* Sometimes, the shows are in colour, sometimes in black and white.

THEY: Sometimes, the show is in colour but the commercials are black and white.

THEM: On *Leave it to Beaver,* Theodore and Wally run the shower but don't get in. They let it run and then splash their hair to make it look wet.

THEY: My sister and I do the same. Standing in the bathroom in bathing suits, I turn on the shower. The bathroom fogs from the hot steam like a sauna. We stand, listening to the water hiss. We pull faces in the mirror. After a few minutes, we splash water on our hair and tell Mum we are done.

*Beat.*

One day, all the black and white ads are gone. Everything is in colour now.

*Beat.*

THEM: Our class digs a hole and puts a time capsule in the school yard.

THEY: There is a 45 record of "Kung Fu Fighting."

THEM: A *Tiger Beat* magazine with Leif Garrett on the cover.

THEY: A school pennant and a basketball.

THEM: On the metal canister it says,

BOTH: 1975.

*Beat.*

THEM: When Mum works till six, we go to the after-school program. The counsellors are high school boys from George Vanier, the tough, cool school where Alex the guitarist from Rush went. One counsellor is super cool and wears sunglasses all the time. He is in Grade 13, for the second time, and is twenty years old. He plays the guitar. He likes me, but not as much as he likes a girl named Sharon.

THEY: Sharon is his favourite.

THEM: She is budding into a woman, he says.

THEY: I am jealous. They hold hands and *she* gets to sit on his knee.

THEM: He has a crush on her and calls her by her last name.

THEY: She is always the star of the annual play.

THEM: Except for one year, when I am Ebenezer Scrooge.

THEY: Good job, Rae, he says.

THEM: He says he likes Sharon best. He says she can be prissy. I am jealous. I want to be her. I want him to love me.

THEY: He called me by *my* last name.

THEM: But I am not a girl. I don't get to play Dorothy.

Eric Blais (Them), Theatre Projects Manitoba, March, 2019.
*Photo by Leif Norman.*

THEY: I play the Wizard.

THEM: It's really my show, not hers. It's called *The* Wizard *of Oz*.

THEY: After the show, he waits outside the GIRLS dressing room to hug her. He wears sunglasses. He is twenty.

THEM: The counsellors talk about breast buds and hairy bushes. They know so much.

THEY: She is thirteen, and he is twenty.

THEM: Pay no attention to the man behind the curtain, the Wizard says.

**17.**

THEY: It is the summer our family went to Niagara Falls. At the gift shop Mum buys us pens. Inside the tube of the pen are ten colours, and you click down on the colour you like.

THEM: The pen is orange and fat and says: Niagara Falls.

THEY: There is another pen too: a lady in a sailor bikini. And when you turn her upside down her clothes fall off.

THEM: I don't want that pen.

THEY: But I do.

*Beat.*

THEM: Now that I am twelve the summers seem short. We are back at school. In the library a taller boy steals my multicoloured pen. I want to cry.

THEY: I am twelve and the world is going too fast. My face is red.

THEM: He holds the pen over my head. I reach for it, but I don't jump. Something old in me tells me not to. I strike his cheek.

THEY: He puts my pen in his tight jeans. I can see the outline of his *thing*. Later, when I leave the library, he blocks my way and holds out my pen.

THEM: Did you hit me or slap me? he asks.

THEY: When I answer, my face is burning, and he gives back my pen.

THEM: I have no idea why he asked me that.

THEY: Yes, you do.

*Beat.*

THEM: After school, there is a new counsellor. He has a giant red afro. He wears sunglasses but isn't cool. He brings us to the gym, and we bake brownies in the kitchen and play dodgeball and floor hockey.

THEY: Things are different. There are now girl counsellors for the girls and we are all made to buy deodorant.

THEM: I must stay with the boys.

THEY: Three days a week, the new counsellor lines the boys in a row on the long wooden bench. In shorts, in a long row, like small skydivers ready to leap.

THEM: From the kitchen drawer, we hear the cutlery tray rattle. He pulls out the long wooden spoon.

THEY: Quietly, he walks tall, along the line of boys and me.

THEM: He faces us, tips forward, and strikes hard with the spoon on our bare upper thighs. Sometimes, the bowl of the spoon snaps in the middle, with a dry crack.

THEY: He stops. But there is always more to come.

THEM: The drawer is full of spoons.

THEY: The game is not to cry out. The game is not to cry.

THEM: He is teaching us to be brave. To not be babies.

THEY: But there's bad in it too, because it's very quiet. Three times a week. And sometimes there are bruises.

THEM: We are brave not to tell. We know, without being told, that something in this is sex.

THEY: But one day, when a boy's mum sees his purple legs, she makes him spill the beans. The administrator comes to the gym when we are baking, and the counsellor must leave. We are given a letter to take home.

THEM: I wanted to be mad at the boy who told. But we'd all gotten tired of the game.

**18.**

THEY: Then, I was thirteen. I loved junior high. I loved the book carousel in the library with the Vonneguts and the Zindels.

THEM: My best friend lived there. On the fiction shelf. Her name was Mick Kelly. And she was like a boy. But she was a girl.

THEY: I wanted to be her so badly. To be inside that book. In the hot summer. In the hot South. *In the town there were two mutes and they were always together.* That's how it begins: *The Heart is a Lonely Hunter* that Carson McCullers wrote when she was twenty-three. The book is full of sadness and silence hangs in the humid air.

THEM: But one night it cools. And Mick is on the verge.

THEY: And she puts on a dress and she puts on lipstick. And soon she will be a woman.

THEM: But for now, she is in between.

THEY: And I sat alone and read. And it was my favourite book. Except for my secret book.

THEM: For it so happened, and it came to pass, in that busy year,

THEY: as our bodies erupted,

THEM: like *Lord of the Flies,* we were left to our own devices. The teachers had gone on strike. And it lasted a month. And those parents who were nervous to leave us at home unattended could push us out the door and off to school. A student body with no head, we did busywork and bided the time. And no one died, by sheer luck.

THEY: And inside we began to slowly change.
And the boys mostly would head back home after being pushed out the door that morning, by mothers who worked.
Or by parents who had simply given up.
And so, the library was really a repository for the weak.
For who goes to school unless made to do so?
Or reads a book unless made to do so?
There were girls and me and my secret book.

THEM: And there was no recess. Because there were no classes.
And there was no recess because it was junior high.

THEY: So, when the weather was warm, kids would go outside.
And the girls would sit in circles.
And I was outside too. And outside the circle.

THEM: But there was much talk among the girls
The obvious –
Breasts which began to grow in –
And I knew, instinctively, grew in sore. And periods.
And although on the margins, I knew more about these miracles
than matters closer to home.

THEY: My outside body was like a stone. And a poison rose. And I felt flooded with hormones and shame. I could no longer be calm. Never would my body spontaneously change.

THEM: At fourteen with angry, hateful industry that left me swollen and raw, I said with bitterness:

THEY: You're a man now!

THEM: It was the end of my calm. And I closed my secret book.

THEY: All that spring, I read that book. It had a black cover. And it told you what happened. What was to come. And it showed you, with drawings that filled me with awe, what could happen.

THEM: Because one day, and you certainly did not want it to happen at school.

THEY: Not the start of it, or how it all ends up.

THEM: But the book said: one day, if you were lucky
Your body could make a baby.

THEY: Because the egg would not come out and run red down your leg.

THEM: It would stay in, and you could grow a baby.

THEY: And your breasts would fill with milk

THEM: And I could feed my baby. And what more could you ask of a life?

## SECTION 2
## PUBERTY / PURGATORY

### 1.

THEM: Let's go downtown and throw eggs at fags. Say the boys in my class.

THEY: Why?

THEM: They're having a parade.

THEY: Why?

THEM: 'Cause it's Halloween; it's the only time in Toronto you can dress like a girl in public and not get arrested.

THEY: It's against the law to dress like a girl?

THEM: Duh, Adam.

THEY: Why?

THEM: 'Cause it's perv, Perv.

### 2.

THEM: On the top floor of our apartment building is a Dutch boy. He is older. We play board games in his bedroom while Mum goes to the laundry. He punches me hard.

THEY: He always keeps the lights off. You could barely see the pieces. He rubs the front of his pants.

THEM: When my mother finishes the wash, she comes to get me.

*Beat.*

THEY: When girls like you, people have to tell you. When boys like you, they hit you hard.

THEM: The best part is later they feel bad and treat you extra nice.

*Beat.*

THEY: In Grade 8, we are on the ski trip, and Derek Savine is nice to me.
He lets me play poker. This guy that only hung out with older guys, Grade 11s.
All the girls sit around the table and stare at him.

THEM: And he let *me* play poker. Out of nowhere, just asked. Bold as brass.
Didn't think he even knew who I was.

THEY: Who you gonna tell that to, Addy Poo?

THEM: It makes me look like a big shot, that he would ask me.

THEY: That's not how you mean it tho', is it?
Homo!

**3.**

THEM: At the last supper, in the Book of John, the last of the gospels, and the newest, the *disciple Jesus loved* reclines in his lap. What might it mean that the *disciple Jesus loved* reclined in his lap?

THEY: How do you know when a boy likes you?

**4.**

THEY: Fuck look at her, guys. Jesus. If I had fucking tits like hers, I'd stay in bed and play with my tits all fucking day. Fuck, yeah. She's got the best fucking tits in Grade 9.

THEM: She's nice.

THEY: Nice fucking tits you mean. I'd love a pair like that.

THEM: I'd love to be her.

THEY: What?

THEM: Nothing.

THEY: What did you say?

THEM: Nothing.

THEY: You said you wanted to be her.

THEM: So?

THEY: What the fuck? You said you'd like to be.

THEM: I said if I had a pair of tits like hers.

THEY: What the fuck is wrong with you?

THEM: Forget it.

THEY: You want a cunt or something?

THEM: No. Stop it.

THEY: You do, you want a fucking cunt?

THEM: I don't.

THEY: Say it.

THEM: No. Stop.

THEY: He's gonna fucking cry, the fucking faggot.

THEM: I didn't say I wanted a fucking cunt! I'd rather be fucking dead.

THEY: Well, what did you mean? That you wanted tits but still have your cock?
What the fuck is wrong with you? He's a fucking faggot.

THEM: I'm not.

THEY: Fuck you.

THEM: Don't!

*Beat.*

THEY: He'll live.
He's just winded.
Fuck him! *(Spits.)*

**5.**

THEM: Here, wipe it, there's still blood.
What did they say to you, anyway?

THEY: Nothing.

THEM: What were they talking about?

THEY: Nothing. Really.

THEM: I saw them staring—they were talking about my boobs.
Weren't they?

THEY: I guess.

THEM: Fuck, they're just *tits*. What's the big fucking deal?

THEY: It's complicated.

THEM: Boys are? Try being a girl.

THEY: No, thanks.

THEM: You sure? I think you'd make a nice girl.

THEY: Why?

THEM: You're nice. You're quiet.

THEY: Really?

THEM: You can smile, you know, Adam. I won't bite.

THEY: Okay.

**6.**

THEM: I was fourteen, fifteen, and his pot was better than mine. We smoked it in his bedroom. He lived in my parents' building. He was East Indian and he was twenty. He had a job. We listened to Led Zeppelin.

THEY: We lay on the floor, with the lights off, black light posters on the wall. His track pants were red. He was always hard. For a while I went often. I wouldn't look at his erection. I didn't want to, it spoiled my high.

THEM: One day, his father came home early. He burst in the room and punched him hard in the face. He asked me to leave. He was polite, and said please. When I left my friend, his lip was split. Around the cut, his soft lips began to engorge and swell.

THEY: I never went back.

**7.**

THEM: For three years, I dragged my feet to junior high. And for a solitary semester, before asthma and a hash pipe did in my lungs, I ran.

Every day. Ran with the gym class, one whole mile. Far in front, a bobbing afro always out of reach: Mr. P, the Adored. A former Toronto Argos running back, leading a pack of teenage toughs.

Flashing back to a Glasgow classroom: we were sat according to our marks, the slower kids the furthest from the teacher.

And here I was again, in the unremarkable middle.

Until one special day, when rest and rage and a newfound coffee habit were the right mix to beat a faster, well-liked boy in my first 400-metre race.

On a real red clay track, like in the movies. At the start (with a real live gun that terrified me), I ran my usual and saw him at my side.

And we'd run like that, I knew we would, until he won the race. But suddenly, on this newly painted, red clay track, I had new knowledge.

It came from my body and a bit from his. And the new knowledge said you are going to win. And it was like when they call out the numbers on a raffle ticket and four numbers down, you're moving towards the prize and you hold the ticket harder.

Trackside, the other kids called my name, and girls were there too.

And it felt like another right number was called, and one more after that and I was still in the race, and it seemed inevitable that the final number would also match mine.

But as my legs began to lock, and my breath disappeared, and when it seemed the last number would never be called, it was already over.

I had won the race. And all the stuff that happens, happened.

They pick you up and bounce you and hug you. And kids start whoop whooping and pat your back, and there's funny dancing, and Rae, Rae, Rae, and pounding arms Rae, Rae, Rae and marching Rae, Rae, Rae, Rae.

And the other boy, red-faced and mad at me.

But I wasn't sorry. I didn't want to say sorry. Not that time.

I was taken aside. Me. And when later, I learned the word avuncular, it was a perfect match. This cool cat, Mr. P, in a red track suit, famous and friendly, asked me if I wanted to try out. Try out. Me. For the track team. And I really did. At that moment, I was full of wanting to.

And I ran a race later, like the one I'd just run, and they said yes, that's it, and you're in.

For a few dozen days I was okay, and an okay boy.

*Beat.*

And somewhere in there, I got the idea I wanted to wrestle other boys. To roll around with them, and hold them, and have it not be bad. And I joined the team.

But I was too weak and was quickly pinned. And when the contest was even, I'd wrap a hold on a same-sized boy, and smell the sweat and deodorant, and not want to move. To stay wrapped and knotted, our bare knees sunk in the spongy blue mat.

But after a few quick losses, and when the next match was stalled a minute or more by me, the new weak boy, depressed and mindless, face down on the mat, Mr. P took me aside. And his words were couched, and he said something about intentions, and besides, not being quite up to the task, but again, about intentions, and things being uncomfortable, and it all being best for everyone if I didn't come back.

That was the end of my sporting career.

## 8.

THEY: At the police station they told my parents I was the fifth largest marijuana supplier in the North York School Division. The avuncular police officer called me son and complimented my fifteen-year-old moustache.

Sarah Constible (They), Eric Blais (Them), Theatre Projects Manitoba, March, 2019.
*Photo by Leif Norman.*

THEM: It was the end of the 1970s.

THEY: The first thing my mother did when we got home was force me to shave it off. Appearances. Always appearances. My grandmother blamed the older boys.

*Beat.*

I collected pictures in a scrapbook. Centaurs half man, half horse. Mermen half man, half fish. What do *you* think it means?

THEM: Well – says Adam, fifteen, a drug dealer seeing a shrink – at the risk of sounding Freudian.

THEY: No risk here, son, I'm a Freudian man.

THEM: He smoked a pipe, Dr. Huttoncott; he had a Van Dyke beard. The school recommended him. I think the idea is that there's nothing below the waist.

THEY: That's human? said the doc.

THEM: No genitalia. Like a mermaid. You know, there's nothing there.

THEY: I see, he said, and leaned forward. He really did.

THEM: It's like Ken, I said.

THEY: Ken?

THEM: Barbie's boyfriend. When you take off their pants, they're both the same. Down there. Downstairs. Nothing there. Void. What do you think?

THEY: I think you're right. That's one way to look at it.
Later, he said: you know that the horse would have its genitalia underneath?

THEM: But there's a line where the human ends, and under that, there's nothing. Like, if you bring a knife all the way across the belly and cut yourself.

THEY: How about magic?

THEM: I like magic. Always been fascinated.

THEY: I was just thinking about the idea of sawing someone in half. It's the same idea.

THEM: I've always been witty, the connections come so fast. I had a dream once about cutting a rabbit in half.

THEY: A rabbit? What might the rabbit mean?

THEM: I don't know, I said: Maybe I'm just splitting hares. He stood up and said I didn't have to see him again. I realized later I'd heard the joke somewhere else.

THEY: Doctor's report, twelve lines long. Conclusion: Normal appetites. Conclusion: All's well. Adam's well.

THEM: Jesus wept, said my mother: What about the drug dealing? Did Adam say why?

THEY: He said – said the doctor – that he liked to smoke pot and someone had to sell it.

THEM: It's one thing to smoke it, and another to sell it.

THEY: He thinks that's hypocritical.

THEM: Oh, don't listen to anything Adam says.

# SECTION 3
# **WILDERNESS**

## 1.

THEY: The first inkling I had that my friend was a rapist was when he raped me.

THEM: Sodomy! From the Greek?

THEY: Good guess but no. From Ecclesiastical Latin.
Named after a town in the Bible. A noun that for me doesn't really work as a verb.
Sodomize. Sounds like something you do to your cashmere sweater. Don't wash it yourself, have it professionally sodomized.

THEM: I've always preferred buggering. Sounds like you're busy. Busy as a buggerer. Diligent.

THEY: My rapist is well known. He's in the biz. My mother knows my rapist. My rapist is the kind of gay man elderly women adore.

THEM: He's rugged and masculine in an old movie star way.

THEY: My mother sends me clippings of him that appear in the newspaper. She thinks I'd like to see them. She doesn't know, of course. Some say a mother should know, but I think in this case that's unfair. I don't throw out the articles about my rapist. It's been a few years since she sent one. I don't know where they are.

THEM: It was the early 80s. Everyone was bisexual. Mick Jagger, Bowie, Rod Stewart.
When AIDS hit – before it killed a single gay man, it killed every bisexual in the city. Bisexuals went extinct overnight. A meteor hit. They went poof. You couldn't find one anywhere. Suddenly everyone knew what I knew since being a wee boy: The penis was a filthy weapon. Not to be trusted, for behind it lay a man.

THEY: That fall, my rapist's brother dies of AIDS. Not the AIDS of the new millennium, the AIDS of the last century. A Saint Vitus Day Dance. Goes medieval on your ass. A calendar of plagues: blindness, suppurating sores, madness, and burning, desiccating, mortifying, hellish bloody torment. To witness it is to see what it means to be *racked* with pain. He was a younger, better-looking version of my rapist. He looked like an actor who might sing in a band.

THEM: He was an actor that sang in a band.

THEY: He was twenty-seven years old.

THEM: I have just graduated from high school. Every night I go down to the comedy club and drink for free.

THEY: August, 1983. After drinking for hours at the club, I will walk with my rapist and another comedian to a fancy apartment in a chic downtown Toronto neighbourhood. I have been to this place many times. My rapist is attracted to me. I let him flirt. I let him paw. I don't care. I'm not a prude. This night he has a treat. He breaks pills into our plastic drinks: vodka and diet Coke, a sickly drink. The powder in the pills doesn't dissolve well. It's an upper, he says. I don't believe him. It's the last of the booze, so I drink it. When I wake up, he is buggering me on a bed. The other comic is passed out beside me. The rapist is fucking my ass. I remember thinking: this is what it's like to get fucked in the ass. He is busy. He is into it. I groan to indicate I'm awake now; he keeps going. I groan again: displeasure.

THEM: He hears me all right, but like a child he tries to snatch more candy from the bowl. I squirm and try to turn. I want him to stop. I'm not angry, I feel nothing. It hurts, I want him to stop.

THEY: I remember he indicates with body movement and groans a kind of "okay, okay, I'm stopping." Like a kind of "oh I see, you don't want to be raped, okay, take it easy, I'm stopping, just give me a second. Just give me a second. Just give a second."

THEM: I pass out. I wake up. My rapist is dead to the world. It's seven in the morning. I've had like two hours sleep. I have a job. I sell tickets at the Canadian National Exhibition. It's a summer job.

THEY: I am nineteen years old. I am a teenager.

THEM: The other comic wakes up. He offers to drive me to work. As we leave the apartment, he asks first: "Is your ass really sore?" Yeah, I say. He fucked us in the ass.

THEM: The drive takes a long time. It's hard to sit.

THEY: I don't know who he raped first. I don't know who he raped second. I don't know who he raped longer. I don't know if he came.

THEM: Fuck, the other comic says a few times, moving his butt in the driver's seat. It really, really hurts. He drops me at work. Before I leave the car, he says: we should talk about this.

THEY: We never do. I never see him again, although about fifteen years ago, he popped up on a national commercial. He looked pretty good for forty.

THEM: I don't know what would have happened if it never happened. I don't think it was right for him to do that to us.

THEY: I wish he never did.

**2.**

THEY: Now that it's happened. Now that it's done. Now that he's finished. Finished the rape. You should tell the police, Adam. You really should.

THEM: I just want to forget.

THEY: Come on now, Adam. The boys in blue are all ears, these days. Cops with those short-cropped haircuts. No beards. Fresh-faced, open-faced.

THEM: Step right up and tell your tale!

THEY: And here's the best bit, kid.
Come on in, see, you see, son. Not a gash in sight!

THEM: You're among men. Your secret's safe.

THEY: Trust us, punk.

THEM: None of what you say will be made public.

THEY: None of what you say will be written down.

THEM: Nothing you say here will be remembered.
Believed.

THEY: Just stick your *sorey* ass on this gunmetal chair. And tell us what happened, as much as you remember, which can't be much of anything.

THEM: You're a bit untidy unkempt unshaven unbelievable.
Not saying these digs is the Ritz, son.

THEY: But you're a mess and your breath's like a brewery.
And you smell like:

THEM: Shit.

THEY: How did you get there? What were you doing?
What the fuck were you both up to?

THEM: Rape?

THEY: Rape, says the little faggot.

THEM: Rape! She thinks it's her prom night. You're kidding, right?
Did you hear that?

THEY: We've got a raped one.
Gather round. Gents.

THEM: Relax, son.

THEY: No offence.
They're just interested.
Gather round. It's a slow night.

THEM: Still is.

THEY: But now this:

THEM: A lover's spat has transpired.
On or about the 12th of Never.

THEY: Between this one sitting here.
And God knows who else –

THEM: – what else – that slunk out of the St. Charles Tavern?

THEY: Some Priscilla –

THEM: – or maybe a pirate with a whip?

THEY: This one doesn't look like it leads the dance.
This one's the bitch. This one always lands on its back.

THEM: Quit crying, for fuck's sake.
You're here now, we must finish the job.
You think this is fun for us?

THEY: What possessed you?
To come here of all places.
Disturbing our peace, with this shit,

THEM: this filth, this crap.

THEY: You're old enough to vote, you're old enough to know better than to come here:

THEM: With your phony regrets.

THEY: With your sob stories.

THEM: With your bullshit.

THEY: And your AIDS.

THEM: You look sick.
Not in the head.
Though that goes without saying.

THEY: Too much to drink.

THEM: Too much to dick.
Fuck me, I'm on fire tonight.
Sarge! What's that one in the dress?
On the radio?

THEY: Boy Georgie!

THEM: Do you really want to hurt me?
Do you really want to make me cry?
What the fuck happened to "I want to hold your hand."
I have two kids at home,
and look at all this sick shit.

THEY: No one wants AIDS tonight, son.
So, wash your hands and don't be touching the cups.
No smoking, kid. No smoking. Sorry.
It's all political correctness now.

THEM: Raped!

THEY: Raped, it says!

THEM: Like the hooker that goes to the bank.
And the money's fake.
Counterfeit says the teller.
And the hooker squeals:
I've been raped.

THEY: Raped, were you?
Raped in the back.
Wipe your snot.
What's your name?
Never mind.

THEM: Get your coat and fuck off.

THEY: Take a cab, son, it's late. You're lucky you weren't rolled.
So, count your blessings.

THEM: Aren't you glad you came?
I think she is not.

THEY: Stay out of trouble, laddie.
We'll see you again. You'll be back.

THEM: Raped!

THEY: Jesus.

**3.**

THEM: Months later, in this clean, well-lit bookshop, I scour the latest books on AIDS.
Hot off the presses. The titles are catching. Now the initials come fast: HIV, STD, finally, but not for a while, AZT. I am terrified to get tested and every fever brings more fear. The plague books are at the back, in the gloomy aisle.
Was the aisle truly darker, shadier?

THEY: In shame, we always turn down the light.

THEM: In the Middle Ages, witches were women who had been outcast
for healing the sick. And here now, the *outcast* were dropping low.

THEY: Oopsy.
Woopsy.
Droopsy.
Down.

THEM: The gay flu was going around.

THEY: Swoopsy,
Woopsy
Droopsy
Down.

THEM: By the year that Orwell was famous for:

THEY: AIDS had come to town.

*Beat.*

I am in my twenties now and my goal is to be an alcoholic writer.

THEM: I make it halfway.

THEM: I have lost my appetite, my breath is sick.

THEY: At twenty-three, I am told, if I don't quit drinking, I won't make it to fifty.

THEM: My mum is with me. I lie on a cot. The Addictions Foundation of Ontario. They have pumped me full of Valium.

THEY: I learn if you try to quit drinking cold turkey, you can have a seizure.

THEM: I learn to not quit drinking.

THEY: I learn that Valium is given to calm you and stop the seizures.

THEM: I learn to like Valium.
They tell me I won't make it to fifty.

THEY: *My rapist's brother died of AIDS. He was twenty-seven. He was an actor that sang in a band.*

THEM: They need to take more blood. Always more blood. The leeches!

THEY: Step right up! See the human pin cushions!

THEM: In bohemian ghettos all over Toronto, empty shops are commandeered.

THEY: Free Clinic. Come on in, AIDS tests: while you wait, try your luck.

THEM: Roll the dice, take a chance, push your luck.

THEY: They're bleeding skeletons. One by one. What a rattle. What a racket.

THEM: Bleeding them dry. One by one.

THEM: Wee boys lining up at pay phones –

THEY: *Their sob stories, their AIDS.*

THEM: – to tell their mums and dads.

THEY: Oopsy, whoopsy,
Dropsy, down

THEM: A husha, a husha.
They all fall down.

*Beat.*

THEY: At the Addictions Foundation, the blood lab is in the building next door, so Mum waits and they take me over. The nurse is kind.

THEM: It is January 5th, 1987. A New Year's hangover has brought me here.

THEY: January 5th, 1987. I've remembered for a reason.

THEM: Margaret Laurence has died. At ten-and-fifty years old.

THEY: She drank quite a bit, says the nurse. You don't want to end up like her.

THEM: Don't I?

THEY: If you want to, she says, we can test you for HIV too?

THEM: I don't. I can't.

*Beat.*

THEY: The nurse takes me through a ward. Shrivelled men schlumply sit in bunchly broken rows.

THEM: One poor soul, hollow eyed –

THEY: *When people drown, we call them souls.*

THEM: – I can smell his breath. Sweet and old. He takes my wrist. His calves are too thin to hold up socks. He leans in, a dusty whisper: They said if I didn't quit, my kidneys would fail.

THEY: *The chorus of men nod in unison. Ghosts of Christmases yet to come.*

THEM: He looks at me with downcast eyes.

THEY: *Vinegar eyes.*

THEM: His bony index taps my sternum: Know what I told them, son?

THEY: I didn't.

THEM: There's always dialysis!

*THEM wheezy laughter and THEY tuts.*

In the midst of death, we are in life,

THEY: Etcetera.

## 4.

THEM: I have given up on writing. I am an alcoholic comedian now. Edinburgh, Autumn of '89.

THEY: Rodney Radcliff, comedy and popular music impresario, has taken a shine to my young self. Had a real nose for talent he did.

THEM: Quite the roster! Manager of The Specials and The Damned.

THEY: Which are you, Addy Poo? Special or Damned?

THEM: Look at me, barely a pup, doing the rounds, shaking hands with Rodney's pals:
Elvis Costello, Shane McGowan.

THEY: Pleased to meet you, gents, says I,

THEM: opening another can of lager.

THEY: Is that Alan Bates with his hand on your back, Addy Poo?

THEM: I would have let him prod me, if he'd wanted. I wasn't a prude.
If he'd wanted.

THEY: Which he didn't. Early call.

THEM: And wife.

*Beat.*

Later, doing the Tourist Rounds of Rainy London: William Blake's House, Bleeding Heart Yard.

THEY: Up there, look. Once, on that very top floor, of that very old building, right fucking there, the real Fagin, the real Dodger plied their trade. I take a snap and wind the spool. I am drunk, wet, and alive.

THEM: And then, turning my eyes downward, I see, lining the sidewalks, huddled in bunches, shivering cold, atop the plague pits where thousands of nameless bones congeal, teenage junkies with bone sunk eyes, stubby teeth and skin like pink paper.

THEY: *He healed the sick with sawdust hands.*

THEM: Among the filthy blankets, the candy wrappers, the fag butts, the crisp bags, and crushed cans of lager, there among the human rubble, tucked in an arm bone cradle, a baby cries, its eyes smeared shut, its mouth agape, a pink, plump mole.

THEY: A pink, plump mole, in lonely London town.

THEM: Oopsy.
Woopsy.

THEY: Droopsy.
Down.

THEM: A husha, a husha

THEY: We
All
Fall
Down.

**5.**

THEM: I tear pages out of my life. Redacted. Blacked out. Not with a pen but with drugs and booze. You can cover up the facts, but the feeling can't be torn out.

*Beat.*

Honestly, I don't remember.

THEY: Honestly you don't remember, or you don't remember honestly?

THEM: Is there a difference?

THEY: You tell me. *Faggot!*

*Beat.*

THEM: Back in Toronto, sick, in fear and hate. My sex life is a failure.

THEY: My life and sex a failure.

THEM: In the midst of death. A failure.

THEY: A failure at life. A failure at death.

THEM: *Alone in the wilderness, the tempter came.*

THEY: *Too much to drink, too much to dick.*

THEM: *What part of myself is my himself?*

THEY: *I close my eyes and bear down. No hope, no tears.*

THEM: Drunk in a bar at noon, I turn to my friend and offer him fifty bucks to kick the shit out of me.

THEY: He declines. He knows I hate myself.

THEM: And never have fifty bucks.

*Beat.*

THEY: I love me, I love me not. I love me, I love me not. I love me not.

THEM: I blink my eyes, on and off, on and off, on and off.

*Beat.*

The comedy boom keeps me in cash. Lots of opportunities

THEY: to drink: In Montreal, the bars were open till four.

THEM: And when the club was short of money, they paid you in coke.

THEY: It was three in the morning and the bar was in the hotel, so what's the harm and I did see the boots in the next stall but what's the chance and then I heard the walkie-talkie and when I came out my nose all white and saw the beard I thought security guard but no cops had beards now and he said where's the coke and I handed it to him and everyone said that was dumb, and then it was three days of them sticking their nose thru the cell door bars and saying how's your high now *anglaise* and then months later back for a trial and the same cops friendly now, and the expensive lawyer and the new Crown attorney's first day, welcome aboard *madame,* thank you judge, and the cops saying possession of half a gram and me saying to the lawyer I did like ten lines before I got pinched, and it was a half gram to start with, and he says I guess you got a good deal *anglaise,* and the Crown attorney saying not worth the bother this one, and the judge saying they should all be this easy, and the cops shake my hand, and keep your nose clean, and stay away from the trouble and I sure will, I lie.

*Beat.*

Then, remember, two weeks later, playing a college gig.

THEM: Same old, same old.

THEY: This was different, Alley Poo. It was the bad coming out.

THEM: *My mother rubbed my elbows. Psoriasis, warts.*

THEY: There was the woman in the audience.

THEM: Redacted, blacked out.

THEY: She had offbeat good looks.

THEM: I didn't say that. Just that I thought she was beautiful

THEY: Just told her. Bold as brass

THEM: She was thrilled. I thrilled her.

THEY: And then after the show.

THEM: A bad show. Lousy crowd.

THEY: You saw her again. You went over, Adam.

THEM: Not sure we need to go into that?

THEY: No?

THEM: I was drunk. I looked at the other comic I was with. I said watch this:
It was a joke. I wanted to make him laugh.

THEY: Did he?

THEM: Yes, it was a joke.

THEY: You saw her again, this girl.

THEM: I saw her again and went over

THEY: Right up to her. The girl you liked? The girl you wanted to be?

THEM: I said.... But I was kidding.

THEY: You said that. You said: I was kidding. You said.

THEM: I said: when I told you before you were beautiful, I was kidding.

*Beat.*

I tried to take it back....

Her friends stepped in they wouldn't let...

THEY: Not their fault.

THEM: That look on her face. It was painful

THEY: Far worse for her.

THEM: I tried...

THEY: To undo the done.

THEY: When holding a knife…
Always point the blade inwards, it's safer.

**6.**

THEY: Every day, curiouser and curiouser, I go to the library and go through heavy, worn-out medical books, I thirst for a knowledge of freaks like me: the human bestiary, living centaurs. Modern mermaids.

THEM: In the old medical textbooks: The patient's eyes –

THEY: *Windows of the soul.*

THEM: Are redacted. Blacked out.

THEM: Here in clinical black and white, behind the library counter, is the hidden life I ache to know. Medical names; Pseudo hermaphrodite, *Psychopathia Sexualis,* Transvestite, Transsexualism

THEY: Here, be dragons. Nature's middle men.

THEM: And middle maids.

THEY: Tits and cocks.

THEM: Beards and cunts.

THEY: Medical sideshows.

THEM: Is this who? Is this what I am?

THEM: Which part of myself is *that* self?

**7.**

THEY: Here are my feelings. And there is this name: transsexual.

Sarah Constible (They), Eric Blais (Them), Theatre Projects Manitoba, March, 2019.
*Photo by Leif Norman.*

THEM: Is this my story?

THEY: Told and sold, in brown paper bags, at the back of porn shops?

THEM: Trannies, He-shes, Ladyboys? Fifty bucks a magazine!

THEY: A terrifying, thrilling, shining pageant.

THEM: This is my heraldry, honour, history and language. Hidden.

THEY: Shit upon with their filth. My history, my secrets, marked up and sold back to me.

THEM: Regifted as perversion and shame.

THEY: Stamped with their stink, I no longer recognize my scent.

THEM: How will I ever find my way home?

## 8.

THEM: Every fever spike, every blood-specked spittle.
Every bubbly tummy, and small bout of the runs.
For ten years, I'm too scared to get tested, to discover if my rape was a homicide.
For ten years, my doctor's waiting room in Toronto's Greektown is an antechamber of skulls.

*Beat.*

THEY: Ten years is a long time. Enough death to last a lifetime.

*Beat.*

THEM: From twenty to thirty years old, I grew in no way

THEY: but tired.

## 9.

THEM: In 1994, I move from Toronto to Winnipeg. I have a partner now. And a child.
I must complete twenty-eight days in a rehab. I am skeletal thin, 116 pounds, the result of drinking twelve ounces of alcohol and six pints of beer a day.

THEY: I drink between 2 a.m. and 5 a.m. in the office of the radio station where I work. I am never drunk on the air, but I am drunk at work. I never get in trouble.

THEM: They take a lot of blood in rehab. Here's the stuff I *don't* have: AIDS, Hep A, B or C, diabetes, cirrhosis. Here's what I *do* have: Moderate liver damage. Tearing of the esophageal lining. My rehab roommate has Hep C. He was a big shot businessman making 150k a year to do a boring job.

THEY: He liked to undo his cufflinks and roll up his suit sleeve, so he could inject a mixture of cocaine and speed into his arm while commuting.

THEM: He's an extrovert. The hepatitis he got is the bad kind. He just got married and now he might need a liver transplant. I'm lucky.

THEY: The rehab is near where my rapist works. Sometimes I see him. He talks to me. I tell him I'm in rehab. He says he will come and see me. He never does.

THEM: By the second week in rehab I am 126 lbs. I have gained ten pounds, but my pants still don't fit. Puncturing my belt with a paring knife, I always push it towards me.

THEY: Always present the smooth handle to the world.

THEM: They force meat down our burning throats to ruddy us up.

THEY: To drink so much and always be parched.
This shall be your punishment from the gods.

THEM: Dip the sponge in vinegar.
Sour wine.

THEY: Would you drink that much water? Would you, Adam?
You're bloody hopeless.

THEM: When my mum and dad get to the door of the treatment centre, the dog runs to greet them. New people don't bother him.
Every twenty-eight days a new batch of men. Every twenty-eight days. Like a period.

THEY: Another group of men. They never ran out. Always a new group of sad-eyed men.
Sad, slumped. Not much to look at. Not much there. Eyes cast down. Vinegar eyes.

THEM: That's how I think of men.
*Guys* you hang out with.
I'm seeing a new *guy*. Bring your *guy* along.
But it's men that get beat down. Men lining up for food. Men lining up for jobs. Men who are weak. Men who don't live up. Men leave.

THEY: My grandfather, as a very good example, left my grandmother alone with two little girls. One of them, my little mother.
One day he was gone. Just up and gone.
They said it was lung cancer.
No excuse.

THEM: Inside the door, looking around, trying not to look around, my mother said:
A place like this should have a dog:

THEY: Okay, get him off me.
Adam! Bloody hell! Adam, get him down!

THEM: I'm trying.

THEY: Well, you're not trying hard enough.

THEM: So, anyway,

THEY: Oh, God, here it comes.

THEM: The counsellor says it's helpful for recovery if you guys come to a family session.

THEY: Oh, *great*. It's always the *mother's* fault.

# SECTION 4.
# **EPIPHANY/INTERLUDE**

## **1.**

THEY: Yesterday, when I was a boy, I met you.
But years before, when you were in high school, the kind of mildly bad girl I pined for, you partook in a low impact traffic accident between two *vehicles* not far from your school.
A minor incident – no one was remotely hurt. But you. The crammed-in kid, small, back seat middle. You *wanted* to wear a seatbelt, but there was none – there were not enough – life preservers.
So, when one car hit the other, stopped it in its tracks, you kept going, past the windshield, and down the street.

And you said – we all say – not my face – please not my face. And you got that wish.
But you split your head in two: emotionally; emotionally.

But you went to sleep right away – if you remember – which you don't – you went to sleep right away – for a whole year – everyone else kept going – as you slept it off – came to a rest, not even a period – everything stopped.

When you finally came to your senses you were quite the unicorn. Still smart, still funny, still sweet, none the worse for wear – a miracle, the doctors said: no one had come back from a coma this far, this well, got this well – well, well, it was just quite something: but emotionally; emotionally.

## 2.

When I came along, I didn't notice at first, how odd you were.
I was in a place, a lonely place. We did it all on impulse, propelled by impulse.
I was patient, so patient with you, until I wasn't. And when I wasn't, I terribly wasn't, I shamefully wasn't.

You did not have to work; your cash settlement was fulsome. You were generous to a fault. You should not have tried to change your will and leave all the money to my daughter on our two-week anniversary. We should have had no talk of two-week anniversaries, in the same way I should not have been mixing Prozac with booze, in the same way I should not be a boy, in the same way I should not be here,
in the same way my wife wants me home, wants to try again.

And AIDS was everywhere and that was your passion, to organize fundraisers for a hospice. And how you treated those dying men, and how you treated me having been raped at nineteen and thinking I might have AIDS too.

But we were safe, that was part of your cause, being safe, always be safe, always wear a seatbelt.

## 3.

How mean people were – she just talks fast – very fast – so what?
She's passionate —They're not lies – she's imaginative – but me,

I was patient.
Until I wasn't.
Nothing lasts.
But my terrible guilt.

How you loved comedy. So, when I moved to Winnipeg, my marriage repaired by denial and hope, my dysphoria dulled by grief and work, I got a call from another ex of yours. And your ex said you were at Just for Laughs and you had met a cast member from *Saturday Night Live,* and you had manically transformed a brief encounter into evidence you were getting married.

The ex said you were in a wedding dress and were wandering the hotel hallways (like a ghost, I remember thinking) and that you had a bottle of champagne.
And so far, no one had called the cops. And I said: Please, I just don't want anyone to laugh at her. And he said: it's not your problem. He said: I just thought you should know.

Then, one day, it was the end of the twentieth century. Now email was invented, so the next time, there was no call from your ex. Just an email.

And it was my birthday. In the subject line: sad news about, followed by your lovely name, Miranda.

And I see now, it can't have been my birthday, it was the day after my birthday.
It was on my birthday, the day before, that it happened – that you leapt off the platform as the subway train came to a *screaming* halt – you kept going, past the rim of the platform, through the air.

There was no grave. No marker, no way to say:

Oh god, I am just so fucking sorry. I am just so sorry, oh god I am, oh god I'm so so sorry.

Oct 1st, 1999. you died on my birthday. I was thirty-five.

You were sixteen when you went through the windshield.

One day, everything is so long ago.

## 4.

This is how it ended:
Working in Toronto, ten years later, 2009.

It was preternaturally cold, and steam rose from the grates of the subway and the trains roared by under the clanking metal plates and screamed to their halt.

On the street, on the sidewalk, there was a man. His coat was too small, and he was blind. His voice was preternaturally high, and his hands, which I took in mine, were preternaturally soft and his eyes were hollow and dark.

He was blind from AIDS. He seemed to have stepped out of the past.

Her past.

I saw that he had sores. I heard his chest. Like a ghost, I remember thinking.

But he was no ghost. He was a man. He was simply poor. He had gotten diagnosed too late. Had gotten and taken medicine too late. Had done everything too late.

I took off my coat. It was new, and it was nice, and I gave it to him.

And by happy chance, it was per diem day at the place I was working. And I had an envelope full of cash.

And I took it out and put it all in his soft hands. And his fingers felt that it was a lot of bills and he said: what are they, so that I know? So I don't get taken advantage of.

And I said: touching the first bill, this is a hundred and he laughed like I was joking. And I said it is. And his body shook. And this? A hundred. And this a hundred. And a fifty and a twenty. And so on. And he was really crying.

And he said a lot of thank yous, and then he said: What is your name?

And I told him hers. I told him her name. And he registered no confusion and he said softly to me: Thank you, Miranda.

And I looked up. It was corny, but I looked up, at the sky, at the stars.

And whatever it was that was in me, that *gnawed* at my gut, since she stepped off that platform – whatever shape it held, it fled.

As when Jesus cast the demon out.

Whatever it was fled.

And the steam rose from the subway, and it was very cold. And he stood there clutching the money and I was about to say you should put it away – when he did.

And I walked back to my rented apartment. And I moved to pull my coat tighter but I didn't have one.

And I turned back to look, and he was gone.

## SECTION 5.
## **REDEMPTION**

### 1.

THEM: I lie on the bare floor and breathe in the past. The bathtub overflows with dishes and fruit flies dance like motes over a bruised and deflated peach. Beethoven's 3rd blaring from my stereo can be heard down the street. I am too high to turn it down. Leaning towers of paperbacks tip like vertical dominos and two rats gambol in their cage.

THEY: Two days earlier, newly divorced, cleaning the cat litter for the first time in a month, I have filled the house with chlorine gas. It rises fast as I carelessly dump bleach and another household cleaner into a buckling plastic litter box. Dark wet sticky clumps, like a ruined city of sandcastles, swirl with white smoke. I drag the rats' cage to the bedroom, grab the cat and take hurdling strides down to the street. On the phone with poison control, I know my life is toxic. I am a half century old. My wine skin is cracked and leaking. Do not put new wine in old skins.

THEM: I am a cracked bell, a broken heart.

THEY: I make my body sick. My body makes me sick.

THEM: *As he healed the sick with sawdust hands – dead skin cells fall like soft pink rain.*

THEY: I have been sober for over twenty years.

THEM: Except for weed.

THEY: And Tylenol 3s

THEM: And porn.

THEY: I am over a half century old.

THEM: Where were you when Kennedy was shot?

THEY: Chilling in my crib.

THEM: I push down, bear down, shove down. I tear pages from my life

THEY: In shame, we always turn down the light.

THEM: In every living room, in every welcoming home, surrounded by families and friends, I am utterly alone.

THEY: It is the summer of 2015. I am half a century old.

*Beat.*

THEM: One day, everything is so long ago.

*Beat.*

THEY: Jesus said: When you were younger you used to dress yourself and go where you wanted. But when you grow old you will stretch out your hands and someone else will dress you and lead you where you do not want to go.

## 2.

THEM: I had taken three days to decide
If I would transition.
And I knew that it would be hard.

THEY: But I said to myself:
Why don't you do this?

THEM: In that warm summer of 2015, everything and everyone was gone.

THEY: I marched through life.

THEM: No heart, no soul.

THEY: Some lines from a poem by Yeats ran through my head:
"I balanced all, brought all to mind."
"The years to come, seemed waste of breath."
"A waste of breath, the year's behind."

THEM: In balance with this life, this –

*Beat.*

THEY: Why don't you do this?

*Beat.*

THEM: My outside body was like a stone. I could no longer be calm.

THEY: I collected pictures in a scrapbook. Centaurs half man, half horse. Mermen half man, half fish. What do *you* think it means?

THEM: A boy on the outside, but never an outside boy.
I just want to be a girl, a girl, a girl, a girl, a girl, girl, a girl....

*Beat.*

THEY: Why don't you do this? I know it will be hard.
But why don't you do this?

THEM: There's no time. like the present. *(Beat.)*
There's no time. Just the present.

THEY: Why don't you do it? Do it, for that child, that child who closed its eyes.
So hard.

*Beat.*

THEM: It will be hard. It will be very hard.

THEY: But you must.

THEM: I must, for that child who closed its eyes.
So hard.

THEY: And I stood in front of the mirror. And I closed my eyes.

THEM: And I said, you must.
And I said my old name.
And I said: but you must.

THEY: You must for that child.

THEM: You must: and out loud
I said: You must.
For *Her.*

THEY: And I opened *my* eyes.

THEM: And out fell the tears.

**3.**

THEM: There are a couple of questions more, Lara, said the psychologist

THEY: And I know you have been very forthcoming and expressed yourself well
But I need these affirmations. For my report. And I know at your age, this must all seem – So, forgive me but I must: Now you know that you will get this gender confirmation surgery. And it is quite something what they can do, but I need you to state for the report. And out loud that you understand that after this surgery
You cannot have a baby. I'm sorry for doing this, but I need you to say –

THEM: I do understand, I say, and she smiles. Until I add: Because I am fifty-two, so
Getting preggers is not very likely! And during her long frown
I quickly add: And I will not be given a uterus. Which makes her smile
And continue:

THEY: And do you understand, Lara, she says, looking down. That they will be removing – during this – *procedure* some parts of your body that you have had for a very long time. And in the –

THEM: She adds, like a flight attendant.

THEY: Unlikely event that you grow to regret this decision, that these parts cannot be put back on – reattached.

THEM: And I say, yes. And she smiles. But I add: Well, technically they could
But the function would not be as – And she frowns, and I add, to restore harmony:
Yes, yes, I understand.

THEY: Well then, that is that!

*End of Play.*